INSIDE YOUR BODY

ALL ABOUT THE FLU

MEGAN BORGERT-SPANIOL

Consulting Editor, Diane Craig, MA/Reading Specialist

Super Sandcastle

An Imprint of Abdo Publishing
abdopublishing.com

ABDOPUBLISHING.COM

Published by Abdo Publishing, a division of ABDO, PO Box 398166, Minneapolis, Minnesota 55439. Copyright © 2019 by Abdo Consulting Group, Inc. International copyrights reserved in all countries. No part of this book may be reproduced in any form without written permission from the publisher. Super SandCastle™ is a trademark and logo of Abdo Publishing.

Printed in the United States of America,
North Mankato, Minnesota
052018
092018

THIS BOOK CONTAINS
RECYCLED MATERIALS

Design and Production: Mighty Media, Inc.
Editor: Jessie Alkire
Cover Photographs: iStockphoto; Shutterstock
Interior Photographs: iStockphoto; Shutterstock

Library of Congress Control Number: 2017961758

Publisher's Cataloging-in-Publication Data
Names: Borgert-Spaniol, Megan, author.
Title: All about the flu / by Megan Borgert-Spaniol.
Description: Minneapolis, Minnesota : Abdo Publishing, 2019. |
    Series: Inside your body set 2
Identifiers: ISBN 9781532115837 (lib.bdg.) | ISBN 9781532156557
    (ebook)
Subjects: LCSH: Human body--Juvenile literature. | Influenza--
    Juvenile literature. | Communicable diseases--Juvenile
    literature.| Respiratory infections--Juvenile literature.
Classification: DDC 616.238--dc23

Super SandCastle™ books are created by a team of professional educators, reading specialists, and content developers around five essential components—phonemic awareness, phonics, vocabulary, text comprehension, and fluency—to assist young readers as they develop reading skills and strategies and increase their general knowledge. All books are written, reviewed, and leveled for guided reading, early reading intervention, and Accelerated Reader™ programs for use in shared, guided, and independent reading and writing activities to support a balanced approach to literacy instruction.

CONTENTS

YOUR BODY

AREAS
MOST
AFFECTED
BY THE
FLU

You're amazing! So is your body.

Most of the time your body works just fine.
It lets you go to school, play with friends,
and more. But sometimes you feel sick or
part of you hurts.

Every year, millions of people get sick with the flu. Most get better in about a week. But sometimes the flu leads to more serious illnesses. Your doctor can help treat the flu. But everyone should try to stay healthy and avoid the flu!

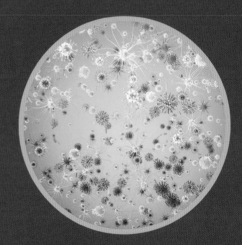

FLU VIRUS

HAVE YOU EVER HAD THE FLU?

ALL ABOUT
THE FLU

Flu is short for *influenza*. This is an **infection**. It is caused by a virus. There are many different flu viruses. They attack your **respiratory** system. This includes the nose, throat, and lungs.

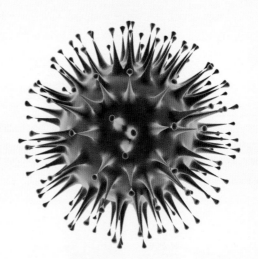

FLU VIRUS

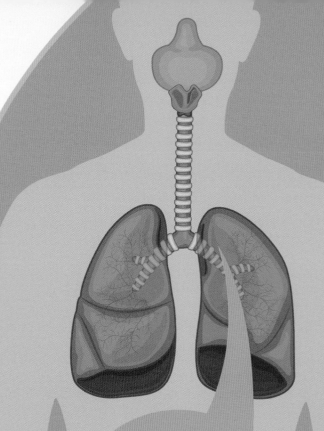

INFLUENZA
(IN-floo-EN-sah)

an infection of the respiratory system

GASTROENTERITIS
(gas-tro-en-
tuh-RYE-tus)

··

an **infection** of the
stomach and
intestines

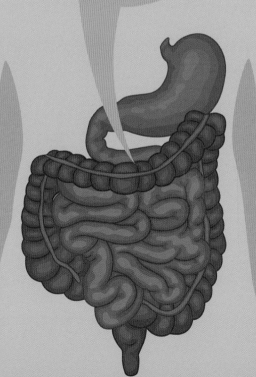

Signs of Influenza

COUGH
SORE THROAT
FEVER
BODY ACHES

Signs of Gastroenteritis

NAUSEA
VOMITING
DIARRHEA

Influenza is not the same as the stomach flu. The stomach flu is called gastroenteritis. Viruses or bacteria can cause this infection. It affects the stomach and intestines.

CAUSES

T he flu is contagious. This means it is easily passed from person to person.

How does the flu virus spread?

SOMEONE WITH THE FLU TALKS, COUGHS, OR SNEEZES.

INFECTED DROPLETS TRAVEL FROM HIS MOUTH INTO THE AIR.

ANOTHER PERSON BREATHES
THE DROPLETS INTO HER
MOUTH OR NOSE.

Flu Season

Flu season is the time of year when the flu is most common. On Earth's northern **hemisphere**, flu season is usually from October to May. The air is colder and drier there during these months. Flu viruses survive better in these conditions.

SIGNS
AND SYMPTOMS

You won't know right away if you have the flu. **Symptoms** begin about two days after you get the virus.

Common Flu Symptoms

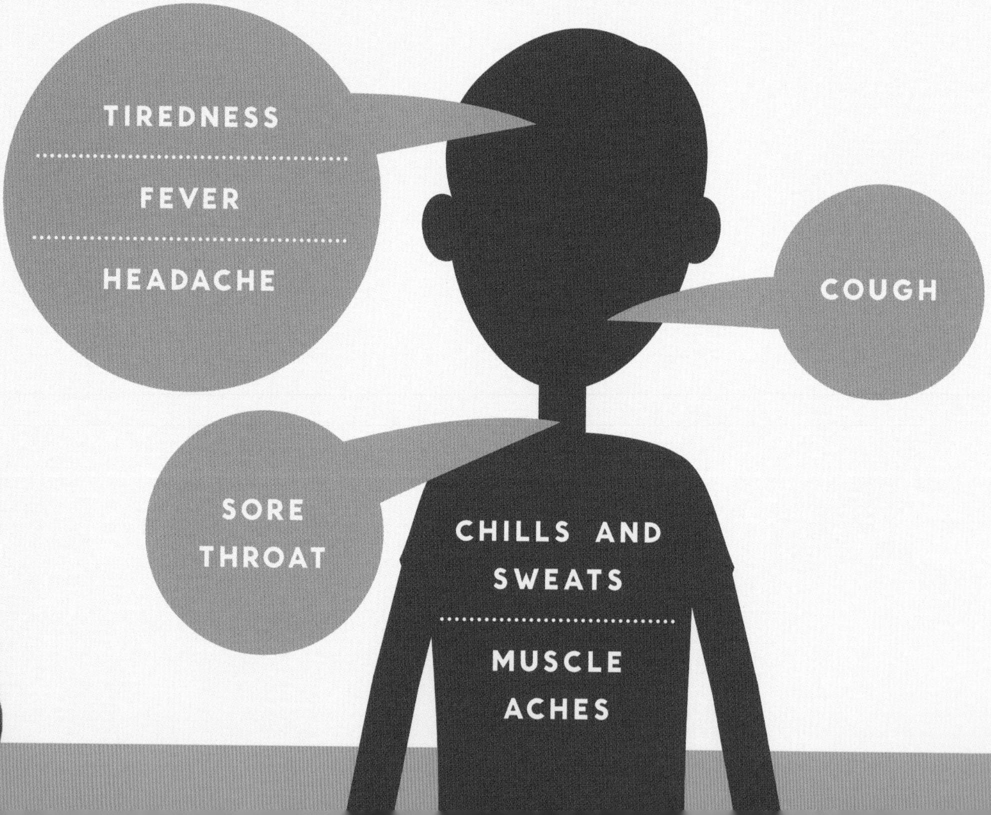

TIREDNESS

FEVER

HEADACHE

COUGH

SORE THROAT

CHILLS AND SWEATS

MUSCLE ACHES

Flu **symptoms** usually last about a week. It is important to stay home from school while you feel sick. You are contagious for five to seven days!

COLD OR FLU

Some people think they have the flu when they really have a cold. This is because these illnesses share common **symptoms**. However, flu symptoms are usually worse than cold symptoms.

COLD

NORMAL APPETITE

RUNNY NOSE

SNEEZING

BOTH

SORE THROAT

HEADACHE

TIREDNESS

COUGH

FLU

LOSS OF APPETITE

FEVER

CHILLS AND SWEATS

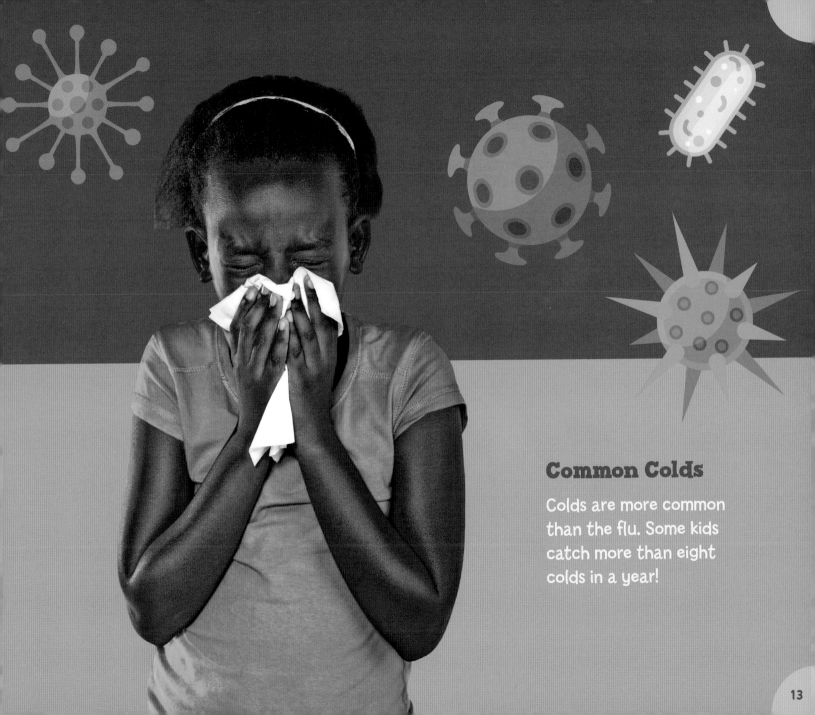

Common Colds

Colds are more common than the flu. Some kids catch more than eight colds in a year!

TREATMENT

Most cases of the flu can be treated at home. It is important to take care of yourself until you feel better.

GET LOTS OF SLEEP. SLEEP HELPS YOUR BODY FIGHT THE FLU.

WEAR LAYERS OF CLOTHING WHEN YOU HAVE CHILLS. IF YOU FEEL HOT, TAKE A LAYER OFF!

DRINK WATER, JUICE, AND SOUP.

There are also medicines and remedies that can ease your **symptoms**.

Symptom	Medicine	Remedy
SORE THROAT	PAIN RELIEVER THROAT SPRAY OR LOZENGES	HOT WATER WITH HONEY COLD FOODS
HEADACHE OR MUSCLE ACHES	PAIN RELIEVER	WARM COMPRESS WARM BATH WITH EPSOM SALTS
DRY COUGH	COUGH SUPPRESSANT COUGH DROPS	HOT WATER WITH HONEY BREATHING STEAM
COUGH WITH MUCUS	COUGH EXPECTORANT	HOT WATER, TEA, OR SOUP BREATHING STEAM
STUFFY NOSE	NASAL DECONGESTANT NASAL SPRAY	PEPPERMINT TEA WARM COMPRESS BREATHING STEAM

COMPLICATIONS

Your flu will likely go away without a trip to the doctor. But sometimes the flu can lead to **complications**. It can also cause more serious illnesses.

Bronchitis

Bronchial tubes move air in the lungs. The flu can **inflame** these tubes. This is called bronchitis. It is also known as a chest cold.

Signs of bronchitis: coughing up **mucus**, chest tightness, shortness of breath

Ear Infection

The flu can cause tubes in the ear to swell. Liquid gets trapped in the ear. This causes **germs** to grow. The germs can **infect** the ear.

Signs of an ear infection: ear pain, trouble hearing, ear drainage

Sinus Infection

Your sinuses are open spaces in your skull. The flu can cause liquid to get trapped in these spaces. This can cause an **infection**.

Signs of a sinus infection: pressure around eyes and cheeks, yellow or green **mucus** from nose, bad breath

Pneumonia (noo-MOW-nyuh)

A flu virus can cause pneumonia. This is an infection of the lungs. It causes liquid and mucus to build up in the lungs.

Signs of pneumonia: coughing, chest pain, trouble breathing

GOING TO THE
DOCTOR

Flu **complications** are more likely to occur in certain people. These people usually have weaker immune systems.

• Kids younger than 5 years old

• Adults older than 65 years old

• Pregnant women

• People with **chronic** medical conditions or diseases

These people should go to the doctor if they think they have the flu. The doctor might give them antiviral medicine. This medicine helps reduce the risk of more serious illness.

When to Call

Call the doctor if you think your flu has caused **complications**. If you have any of these **symptoms**, go to the doctor right away!

• Fever with a rash

• Trouble breathing

• Bluish skin color

• Flu symptoms that get better and then get worse

FLU VACCINE

The flu vaccine can help protect you against the flu. It is often called the flu shot. There are important things to know about this vaccine.

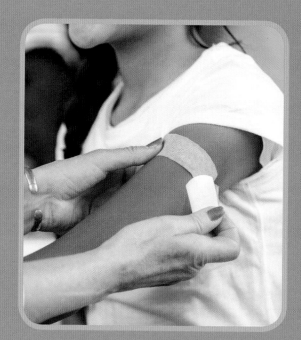

Q: How does it work?

A: The flu vaccine is given as a shot. The shot gives you a small dose of flu viruses. But the viruses won't make you sick.

Q: How does it help?

A: The flu shot exposes your body to viruses. This prepares your body to fight the flu. You might still get the flu if you're vaccinated. But your **symptoms** will be milder.

Q: Who should get it?

A: Babies, kids, and adults should all get the flu shot. It is important that people at risk for flu **complications** get the shot.

Q: When should I get it?

A: It's best to get the flu shot before flu season starts. This gives your body time to build up immunity to the viruses.

Q: How often should I get it?

A: Flu viruses are always changing. So, the flu vaccine changes too. You should get a flu shot once a year. This protects you from each year's viruses. And it keeps your immunity strong!

PREVENTION

The flu shot is the best protection against the flu. But you should always practice healthy habits. This helps prevent you from getting sick. Follow these steps to fight off flu viruses and keep them from spreading!

KEEP A SAFE DISTANCE FROM FRIENDS AND FAMILY WHO HAVE THE FLU.

DON'T SHARE CUPS, SPOONS, OR FORKS WITH ANYONE WHO IS SICK.

COVER YOUR MOUTH AND NOSE
WITH A TISSUE OR SLEEVE WHEN
SNEEZING OR COUGHING.

WASH YOUR HANDS BEFORE AND
AFTER TOUCHING YOUR EYES,
NOSE, OR MOUTH.

USE WARM WATER AND SOAP TO
WASH YOUR HANDS.

DON'T GO TO SCHOOL IF YOU HAVE
THE FLU. REST AT HOME UNTIL YOU
FEEL BETTER!

CHRONIC - when something occurs frequently or for a very long time.

COMPLICATION - a second condition that develops during the course of a primary disease or condition.

GERM - a tiny, living organism that can make people sick.

HEMISPHERE - one half of the earth.

INFECT - to enter and cause disease in. The resulting disease is an infection.

INFLAME - to cause swelling, redness, and pain.

MUCUS - a slippery, sticky substance produced by the body.

RESPIRATORY - having to do with the system of organs involved with breathing.

SYMPTOM - a noticeable change in the normal working of the body.

GLOSSARY